Mel Bay Presents

Early American Roots

VIOLIN EDITION

Transcribed and edited by Geoff Wysham
Music compiled by Tina Chancey

HESPERUS

Early/Traditional Music Ensemble

Country dance tunes, improvisations
& shape note hymns from British Colonial America—
from the arrival of the first colonists
to the American Revolution
and the birth of our Republic.

To contact Hesperus:
3706 North 17th Street, Arlington, VA 22207
(703) 525-7550 • www.hesperus.org

The tunes from this book can be heard on the Maggie's Music recording, *Early American Roots* (MM216).
It is available on compact disc. For more information regarding this and other recordings and books, and to
receive a free Maggie's Music catalog contact:

MAGGIE'S MUSIC, PO BOX 490, SHADY SIDE, MD 20764
(410) 867-0642, WEBSITE http://www.maggiesmusic.com

Maggie's Music recordings and music books are also available from Mel Bay Publications. *Early American Roots*
is also available in versions for flute, whistle, recorder, hammered dulcimer, and cittern from Mel Bay.

1 2 3 4 5 6 7 8 9 0

Visit us on the Web at www.melbay.com — E-mail us at email@melbay.com

Contents

Acknowledgements

We would like to thank Maggie and the staff at Maggie's Music, particularly Connie McKenna, for all their help and encouragement. And for his diligence, tolerance and attention to detail Geoff Wysham deserves unbelievable riches, tremendous happiness and showers of praise. The first book is always the hardest, Geoff.

Here's What They're Saying...

About *Early American Roots*

[On Tina Chancey] "Playing this energetic, rhythmically vivid homespun music and comparing it with the elegant music written for the French aristocracy, you get a precise idea of what is meant by the term 'crossover.'"
—Joe McLellan, WASHINGTON POST

"When musicians speak of 'roots music,' they're generally referring to tunes three or four decades old. When Hesperus invokes the term, [it is] probably referring to tunes three or four centuries old. Its new album is a delightful case in point, brimming with melodies coined centuries ago…lively country dances and graceful cotillions juxtaposed with the often stark and solemn hymns. Still, Hesperus manages to cast an unbroken spell…improvisations seem natural and seamless…it's the trio's nimble balancing of fidelity and freedom, more than anything else, that makes this musical history tour so consistently appealing."
—Mike Joyce, WASHINGTON POST

"[On Scott Reiss] Among American recorder players, his quality is more vocal and more naturally communicative, Reiss "sings" his way through a marvelous collection…Reiss's playing of hammered dulcimer adds yet one more texture to a set of already wonderfully varied improvisations and realizations."

"Wonderfully varied improvisations and realizations…a marvelous collection."
AMERICAN RECORDER

"…A marvelous record. It has such a fresh sound and is extremely well played…."
—David Brower, *Music Director, KRWG, New Mexico*

"…A truly spirited collection which will appeal to a wide audience, from fans of Celtic sound to those who enjoy Baroque classical. A beautiful collection; highly recommended."
—*Midwest Book Review*

"…A trio of musicians whose obvious love of the music shines through exceptional talent filtered through years of playing. These 22 tracks are an outstanding overview of early "American" music as well as a fine jumping off point for those interested in the history of British Isles folk. Essential listening!"
—*JAM Magazine, FLORIDA*

About Hesperus

Hesperus Early Music Ensemble is one of the nation's first and most important performers of "chamber folk" music. While its globetrotting members have impressive credentials as early music performers, the ensemble steps beyond any single genre into a visionary synthesis of living and historic traditions. Its programs embrace eight centuries of music from four continents.

Hesperus consists of six musicians who perform, in different combinations, three kinds of programs: crossover programs fusing European early music with American traditional styles such as blues, Old-time and Cajun; cultural portraits combining early and traditional music such as Early Music from Eastern Europe and Celtic Roots; and single-genre programs of medieval, renaissance, British and Spanish Colonial, and baroque music. Hesperus honors multi-culturalism by tracing the musical traditions of various cultures back to their origins, and then bringing those roots alive in performances wholly its own.

Hesperus has toured the United States, Southeast Asia, Latin America and Europe, and records for Maggie's Music, Koch International, and the Dorian Group. A frequent performer at the Smithsonian Institution in Washington, D.C., the ensemble can be heard regularly on National Public Radio and CNN. *Early American Roots* is the first of a series of "Roots" recordings by Hesperus on the **Maggie's Music** label. Their second release in this series is *Celtic Roots*, Scottish and Irish music from the earliest traditional sources. Both are available from **Maggie's Music**. Hesperus also has eleven other CDs on the Dorian and Koch International Classics labels. For information, see the Hesperus contact information at the beginning of this book.

About the album *Early American Roots*

Early American Roots presents a cross section of popular American instrumental music from before, and just after, the American Revolution. The same instruments that were popular in England in the 17th and 18th centuries accompanied settlers to North America. Recorders and flageolets (the wooden predecessor to the tin pennywhistle) made excellent solo instruments and could be transported in a pocket. The hammered dulcimer (or "dulcimore," as the English called it) required more space, but a dedicated musician found room for it on the first ship to Jamestown in 1607. The violin, the most common instrument for dancing, and the more private viol (viola da gamba) were favorite instruments on both sides of the Atlantic. There is superb solo music for the viol such as the compositions of Tobias Hume, a retired sea captain. The cittern, a popular instrument from Elizabethan and later times, often hung in barbershops for customers to play upon.

Music was used for both private amusement and public entertainment, and reflected the cultural differences between colonial North and South. Southern colonists tried to replicate the gracious life of English country manors. Plantations often employed full-time "dancing masters" so that residents should not "revert to barbarism in the wilderness." One 18th-century traveler to the New World noted that the ladies of Virginia were "immoderately fond of dancing." In contrast, the Puritans in New England at first prohibited dancing but eventually succumbed to its appeal.

The dance music on *Early American Roots* represents two basic genres of dance: country dances and cotillions. The main type of country dance is the line or 'long' dance, with couples dancing in a long double line down the floor. Many of the country dance tunes on this recording are still danced today with original choreography. Cotillions, brought to America by our French allies during the American Revolution, are the predecessors of the modern "square" dance, with two or four couples forming a dancing unit.

Dance music has always been an oral tradition. Musicians played and passed along their tunes by ear. Nonetheless (and fortunately for us) publishers in the 17th and 18th centuries found a large market for printed music among amateur musicians. *The English Dancing Master* was first published by John Playford in 1651 and reprinted many times by his son Henry. It is our most extensive source of English country dance tunes. *Apollo's Banquet for the Treble Violin* was a collection of dance tunes from the latter part of the 17th century.

In America another family of publishers, the brothers Carr, imported Playford prints and published many of their own collections, including the *First Book of Cotillions*. "Daniel Purcell's Ground," "John Come Kiss Me Now," and "Johnny Cock Thy Beaver" (referring to a beaver hat) are all examples of written-out improvisations known as "divisions." *The Division Violin*, published by Playford and imported to America by the Carrs, was one of the most popular of many sets of divisions offered as guides to the amateur player.

Although the three divisions mentioned here were written out, there is much left for the performer to improvise. Before this century, improvisation was an important part of instrumental music performance. In classical music today, it is almost a lost art form. **Hesperus** brings it alive again throughout this recording, improvising the accompaniments to all the dance tunes and divisions, and creating its own versions of "Buttered Peas."

Shape note hymns such as "Captain Kidd," "Nashville," and "The Garden Hymn" are unique to American culture. Singing schools were started in the 1720s to teach parishioners to read music. These schools became an important social outlet for Colonists. The pieces contained in "shape note hymn" books like *Southern Harmony* and *Wyeth's Repository* are truly American, composed consciously to break from European theory and tradition. Their melodies are often stark, sometimes even angular and disjointed, as in the hymn "Rockbridge," but they are nonetheless hauntingly beautiful.

Scott Reiss

How to Use This Book

All the tunes in this collection are playable on a standard-tuned fiddle (violin). The tunes have been arranged in the order found on the album *Early American Roots* as much as possible. Chords are provided to identify the harmonic structure of each piece as well as to give the opportunity for the use of an accompanying instrument, such as the guitar. The chords will also provide information for the advanced player for further embellishments and variations, according to taste. In some cases, the key of a piece has been changed to make it playable on fiddle. In these cases, both the key of the piece and the original key from the album have been listed. Listening to the album will be an invaluable aid in capturing the energy and spirit of this music.

Introduction

Music In Colonial And Federal America

The Oral Tradition

Today, at the end of the 20th century, music is usually separated into classical and popular music. Classical music is learned from written notation, and the written music is often used in performance. Popular music is mostly learned by ear, by listening to someone else play or sing it. Popular performers seldom use written music in performance.

In the 17th and 18th centuries, there was much less of a split between musical styles. Much popular music (including theatre tunes, folk music, ballads, and dance music) originally learned by ear was published in collections for the use of amateurs, people who had the leisure time to learn how to play instruments and read music. In the 18th century, much folk and other popular music was arranged for pianoforte and played in the parlor after dinner. Music publishing was a thriving industry in Philadelphia, New York and Baltimore, and people subscribed to monthly musical magazines which offered new arrangements of all the latest tunes from America and the British Isles.

Some of the music in this book was originally part of an oral tradition but we've had to learn it from books since no one from the 18th century is around to teach it to us. Some tunes have remained part of a continuous oral folk tradition and we've been able to compare the modern versions with the 18th century written ones. Some are ballads, some are dance tunes, some are divisions (variations) on a ground or repeating bass line. Most of them were so well known in Colonial and Federal America that they had the status of common tunes.

Common Tunes

Think of the two hundred or so tunes you know; holiday songs, nursery rhymes, ad jingles, folk tunes, pop songs, camp songs, TV theme songs. These are modern common tunes, tunes almost everyone in our society knows. 17th and 18th century people had an even bigger collection of these 'common tunes' in their heads; perhaps their memories were better because they needed to rely on them more than we do today. 'Common tunes' could be vocal or instrumental. In order to publicize news of the day, great catastrophes, murders, battles and floods, a poem would be written about the incident and printed on a large sheet of paper called a 'broadside' with a notation, "To be sung to the tune of…" and a vaguely appropriate common tune would be named. Sometimes we forget that 'The Star Spangled Banner' was a poem written to the common tune 'Anacreon in Heaven,' the theme song of the Anacreontic Society, a drinking fraternity.

When Common Tunes Are Written Down

When people learn tunes by ear it's a little like a game of telephone; one player learns the tune from another person, he or she then teaches it to someone else, and so on.. And just as details of the story change in a game of 'telephone,' little details of music handed down from player to player change as well. This fluidity has always been a valued thing in popular and traditional music.

When tunes from the oral tradition are written down, both in the past and today, this fluidity comes into play; these written tunes are often just a simplified version, lacking chords or harmony parts, ornaments and instrumentation. Such choices are left up to the player who is expected to make musical decisions according to his own taste and skill, putting something of himself in the performance. In this way, the partnership between the composer (anonymous or known) and the player is closer to 50/50, unlike modern classical music where a performer's interpretation is controlled by a wealth of written dynamics, articulations and ornaments. Listening to the CD can give you an insight into the way in which we add style to this music.

We encourage you to learn and play any of these tunes by ear. It can be very scary to play without music if you've been trained to read it. We still remember the first time we played a concert from memory; it was truly terrifying but it changed our lives. Give it a try.

Ornaments And Divisions

In order to make a tune prettier, alleviate boredom or just plain show off, players would add extra notes to a tune, either writing them down before hand or improvising them on the spot. Extra notes surrounding a single note are 'note ornaments,' including trills (called 'shakes' in England), turns (called 'rolls' in Ireland), and mordents (called 'cuts' in Ireland). Note ornaments are played quickly, decorating the original note with filagree. If extra notes are added connecting two subsequent notes they are 'line ornaments,' including short scales, lower and upper neighbors, passing tones and extending into arpeggios and other figuration. When so many line ornaments are added to a melody that they change the melody into a new tune with rhythms twice as fast, 'divisions' have been made over the melody. For an example of divisions over a melody, listen to 'The Merry Milkmaids' and 'The Ball.'

Divisions can also be made over a bass pattern, chord pattern or 'ground.' One of our modern grounds is 'Heart and Soul.' 'Greensleeves' is a melody written over a ground called the passamezzo antico or Romanesca. In The Division Flute, which is a collection of divisions, really written-down improvisations, we see that the ground was usually divided ten to fifteen times, the sections contrasting in mood.

What To Do With This Music

Any one of these tunes is delightful all by itself. But what if you want to create a little suite of tunes, or use one to accompany a dance, or as background to a dramatic event? Since all you might have is the tune's skeleton, often just the notes of the melody and a few chord suggestions, what do you do?

First you decide on your instrumentation. In the past, people used the instruments they had on hand, producing such interesting combinations as violin and french horn, harp and cello, flageolet and pianoforte. Two or three instruments can share the melody, either by taking turns or playing in unison or octaves. It was common for two sorts of instruments to share the accompaniment, a low melody instrument on the bass line (or making one up if none was given), a cello, viol or bassoon for example; and a chordal instrument to fill out the harmony, a harp, guitar, harpsichord, cittern or pianoforte.

Next, you can create an arrangement. Decisions you need to make include; How many times will you play through the tune(s)? In what order will you play them? In what keys? Do you really like the printed bass line? (You might just leave it out.) How about the chords? Will you create introductions, interludes and postludes (or codas)? Will you change tempos? Perhaps you will change instruments on the different tunes? Third, as you play your tunes through more than once, how will you develop them? Will you add or vary the chords? Divide the bass line? Add a counter melody (a second, independent melody), a line of harmony in another instrument, a descant (an upper independent melody), a drone (sustained pedal point)? Will you ornament the melody with note ornaments, line ornaments or divisions?

The possibilities may be overwhelming! Some people may feel they don't have enough experience with music from the past to make so many performance decisions. If you feel that way, we suggest that you listen to our Early American Roots recording with this book in hand so you can see and hear how we make our own arrangements. None of us can faithfully reconstruct the past, but with care and love we can recreate it. One suggestion: try not to let your arrangement get in the way of the tune. Good tunes live on, they have an energy and character all their own. Now, experiment and enjoy!

Tina Chancey

Techniques

This collection of tunes notates the various embellishments used in the following manner:

Turn - A note with the marking ♩ indicates a turn. It is played ♪♪♪♪ . Where a turn is indicated over a longer note, or where it is indicated after a note, more time is given to the first note of the turn.

Grace note - A grace note is shown as a small note directly preceding a primary note, and is played quickly, as a lead into the primary note.

Half Mordant - A half mordant is marked as ♩ and is played as ♪♪♩ .

You may find it easier to learn a piece without the various embellishments first, adding the grace notes, slides, etc. once you learn the basic tune.

Madison's Whim

Key of D

First Book of Cotillions
arr. © Hesperus

We've put a medley together of (A) "Madison's Whim," (B) "The Merry Strollers," and (C) "The Killerman," because we thought the three jigs had just the right combination of similarity and contrast. "The Killerman" is a particular favorite, not only because it starts like the theme song of "Leave it to Beaver" but because it's a crooked tune; between the first and second sections it seems to add a dotted quarter to the second ending, and then corrects itself at the da capo (the return to the first section). Or does it really do that?

The form is A B A(no repeats) C A(no repeats).

The Merry Strollers

First Book of Cotillions
arr. © Hesperus

Key of G

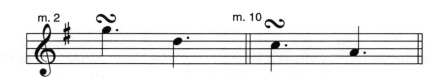

The Killerman

Key of G

First Book of Cotillions
arr. © Hesperus

Bobbing Joe

Key of A dorian

The Dancing Master
arr. © Hesperus

Fiddle Improvisation

Fiddle & Dulcimer Variations

We like to play with the rhythm in this piece; the tune is in 6/8 but the dulcimer and cittern accompaniment, as well as my fiddle counter-melody, are in 3/4. On the recording we "medlecize" this tune and "Cuckolds," "Rufty Tufty" and "Parson's Farewell."

Cuckolds All in a Row

Key of G

The Dancing Master
arr. © Hesperus

Cittern Version

Hesperus

Scott Reiss, Tina Chancey, and Mark Cudek

Rufty Tufty

Key of G

The Dancing Master
arr. © Hesperus

Recorder harmony

m. 1 (of 3rd time)

m. 4 (of 3rd time)

After we play the tune in unison, Scott and I alternate playing the melody,
each making up our own counter-melody and divisions. Do try this at home, kids!

Parson's Farewell

Key of D minor

The Dancing Master
arr. © Hesperus

In our version, we trade the tune from cittern to whistle to viol and back to whistle, getting faster as we go. Notice the slap-bass viol on the fourth time through.

Captain Kidd

Key of A minor

Southern Harmony
arr. © Hesperus

Through all the world be - low, God is seen all a -

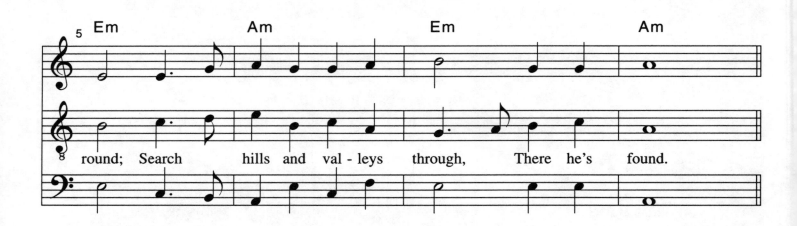

round; Search hills and val - leys through, There he's found.

The grow - ing of the corn, The li - ly and the

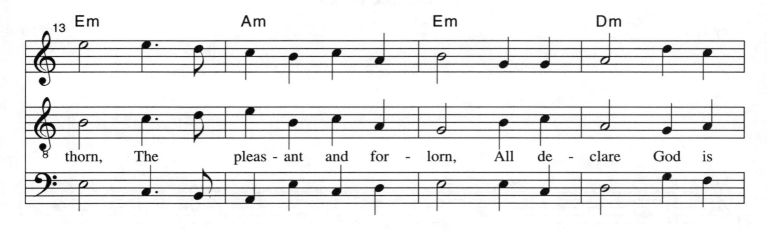

thorn, The pleas - ant and for - lorn, All de - clare God is

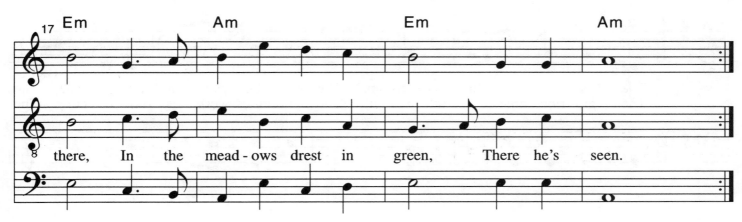

there, In the mead - ows drest in green, There he's seen.

2. See springs of water rise,
Fountains flow, rivers run;
The mist below the skies
  Hides the sun;
Then down the rain doth pour
The ocean it doth roar,
And dash against the shore,
All to praise, in their lays,
That God that ne'er declines
  His delight

3. The sun, to my surprise
Speaks to God as he flies;
The comets in their blaze
  Give him praise;
The shining of the stars,

The moon, as it appears,
His sacred name declares;
See them shine, all divine!
The shades in silence prove
  God's above.

4. Then let my station be
Here on earth, as I see
The sacred One in Three
  All agree;
Through all the world is made
The forest and the glade;
Nor let me be afraid.
Though I dwell on the hill,
Since nature's works declare
  God is there.

Unlike the cotillions, whose accompaniments are just suggestions, these shape-note hymns ("Nashville," "Rockbridge" and the "Garden Hymn" are the others) were originally written in a three-part American-style harmony and counterpoint that was designed to be as different as possible from European parlor music. When you play them, they'll sound most distinctive if all three parts are represented. Remember, if you want to play them with a solo voice and chords, the middle voice is the original melody! Also, if you've got a larger choir of instruments, you'll get a fuller, more typical shape-note sound if you double each part, so that the top two can be heard in soprano and tenor ranges and the bottom in bass and alto ranges. This is often how sacred harp music is sung. Use the words to give you hints on phrasing and articulations.

The titles of shape-note hymns usually refer to the melody's original appearance as a Broadside Ballad; these were the equivalent of newspapers in 17th century England. New words about the scandals and disasters of the day were set to familiar tunes and distributed to the populace on wide sheets of paper called "broad-sides." While the "Ballad of Captain Kidd" described the capture and hanging of the famous pirate, the devotional text is completely different.

Nashville

Key of G

Southern Harmony
arr. © Hesperus

The Lord in - to his gar-den come, The spic - es yield a rich per-fume, The
The glo - rious time is fall-ing on, The gra - cious work is now be - gun, The

spic - es yield a rich per-fume, The li - lies grow and thrive;
gra - cious work is now be - gun, My soul a wit - ness is;

A tune in jig-time (6/8 meter). Many of these tunes originated in Ireland; "Nashville" could have been a type of dance tune popular in County Kerry called a "slide."

A Sett of Hornpipes

Keys of D minor/D aeolian/D major

Apollo's Banquet
arr. © Hesperus

Hornpipe

A New Hornpipe of Mr. *Purcell's*

A Horn-pipe

Recorder harmony for last section

John Playford's "Apollo's Banquet" includes more than a dozen hornpipes and jiggs, as well as round-os (rondos) and minuets. Tina selected and arranged these hornpipes into a set, as well as the jiggs (old spelling) you'll see later.

Butter'd Peas

Key of G

The Fashionable Lady
arr. © Hesperus

Recorder Variation

Fiddle Variation

Cittern Variation

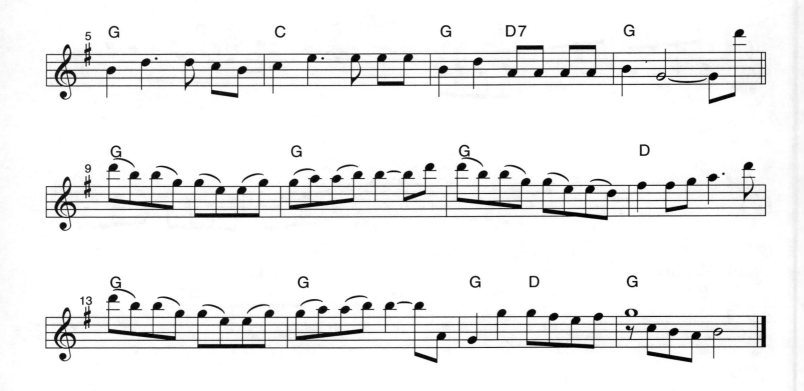

Although the Englishman James Ralph featured this tune in the first American Ballad Opera, "The Fashionable Lady" of 1729, "Butter'd Peas" was originally Welsh and it's still popular in Wales today. We use it as an improvisational framework, each of us taking turns over the simple chord changes.

Daphne

Key of D minor

The Dancing Master
arr. © Hesperus

34

Another common tune, Daphne is found in a plethora of sources, from the 17th century "Fitzwilliam Virginal Book," a fascinating compendium of florid and complicated variations written for a pair of virginals or small harpsichord; to consort song partbooks (many solo songs were accompanied by a consort of viols, something like a modern string quartet with different sized viola da gambas on all parts); to the solo recorder variations written by the blind Dutch musician Jacob Van Eyck. Scott plays a fairly simple version on the whistle.

La Poulle

Key of D

First Book of Cotillions
arr. © Hesperus

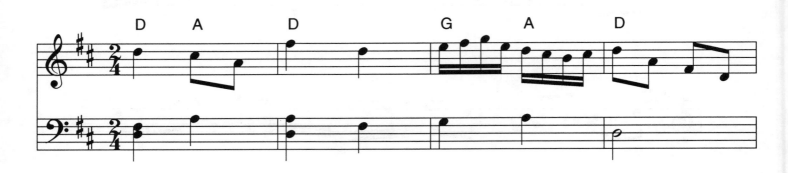

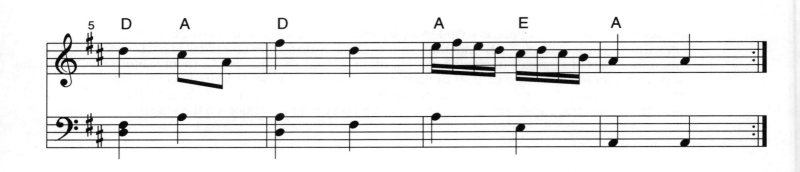

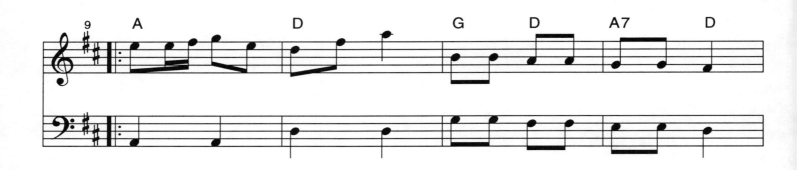

The Cotillion was a French dance, one of the ancestors of our modern square or set dance. Cotillions came to America during our Revolution when the French were our allies. The title means "The Hen."

Childgrove

Key of E dorian

The Dancing Master
arr. © Hesperus

"Childgrove" works well as a dulcimer piece, moving easily from a moody drone number to a rousing dance tune. In its original setting as a country dance tune it would have been played at a constant tempo throughout.

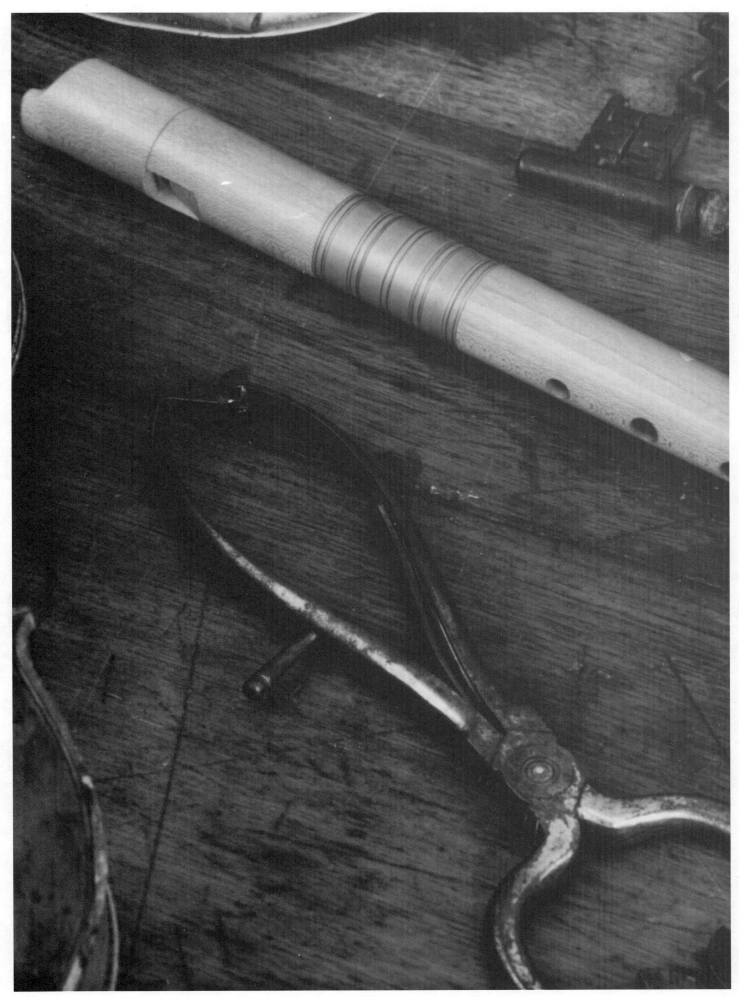

The Spirit of Gambo

Key of D minor

Poeticall Musick/Tobias Hume
arr. © Hesperus

During much of the Renaissance and baroque periods, the bass viola da gamba was the instrument of choice for professionals and amateurs alike. Its rich, resonant tone which can be compared to the human voice; its bow technique which, with fingers on the hair, provided for interesting nuance and subtlety; and the flexibility it had, due to its six strings and frets (like a kind of bowed guitar) to play melody and/or harmony parts ranging from bass to soprano, made it popular with composers such as Tobias Hume. Hume was a soldier who wrote and published two books of viol music in tabulature,

Portsmouth

The Dancing Master
arr. © Hesperus

Key of G

We use the Portsmouth tune in a rondo form, as the recurring glue between the other tunes. Our order is: "Portsmouth," "Staines," "Lusty Gallant," "Portsmouth," "Chelsea," "Portsmouth," and "Argeers" as a coda.

Staines Morris

Key of G minor

The Dancing Master
arr. © Hesperus

Lusty Gallant

Key of G aeolian

The Dancing Master
arr. © Hesperus

Chelsea Reach

Key of G

The Dancing Master
arr. © Hesperus

Argeers

Key of G

The Dancing Master
arr. © Hesperus

Variations

Daniel Purcell's Ground

Key of G minor
Original Key of C minor

The Division Violin
arr. © Hesperus

Smoothly

Ground Bass

Divisions on a ground are fertile playgrounds for improvisation, not only in the solo part but in the accompaniment as well. Divisions can be accompanied by keyboard instruments such as the harpsichord or small organ; plucked instruments, lutes, guitars, citterns and harps; with an added sustained instrument on the bass line if desired—viol, cello or bassoon. Cello and viol, for that matter, can play both bass and chords if desired. Although a simple ground is notated at the beginning of the piece, a real bass line can be created "extempore" to mirror the mood changes of the melody, and the chordal instrument should follow suit. These variations can be written down or left to the drama of performance.

Scott also varied some of the written melody, as well as repeating a fast section closer to the end for balance. With the written music before you, listen to his version of the piece to hear what he changed. As in many other division pieces, such as "Johnny Cock thy Beaver," the ending of "Daniel Purcell's Ground" winds down; a sort of written-in, gradual ritard.

New Jersey

First Book of Cotillions
arr. © Hesperus

Key of G

These two cotillions, "New Jersey" and "The Ball," seem to us particularly American; we think, (anachronistically) of cotton candy and state fairs. While Scott added ornaments on the melodies, Tina added counter melodies to both, giving a ferris-wheel sort of feeling.

The Ball

Key of G

First Book of Cotillions
arr. © Hesperus

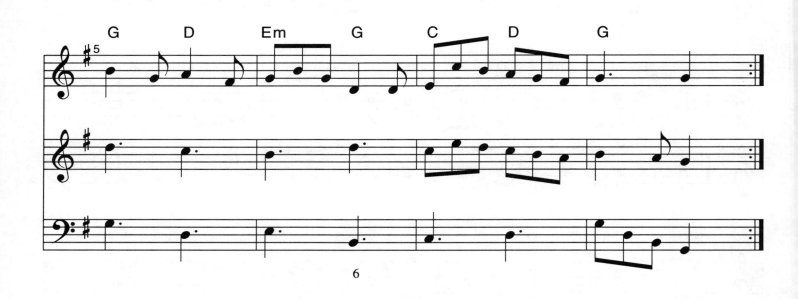

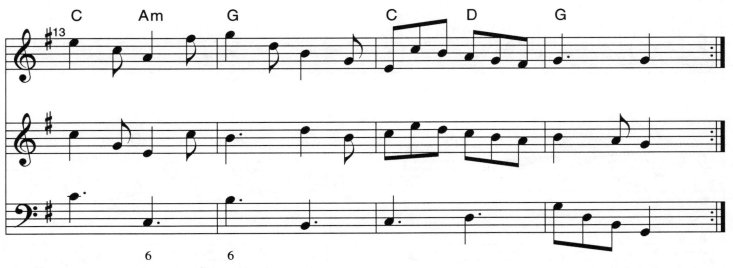

Fully Ornamented Version

54

Rockbridge

Key of C

Wyeth's Repository of Sacred Music, 1820
arr. © Hesperus

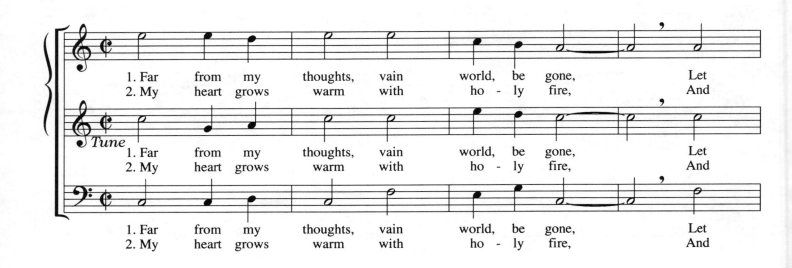

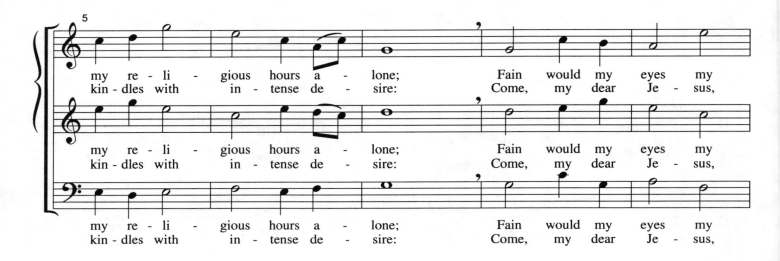

Garden Hymn

Key of G

Wyeth's Repository of Sacred Music, 1820
arr. © Hesperus

Tune

The Lord in-to his gar-den comes, The spic-es yield a rich per-fume,

The lil-ies grow and thrive, The lilies grow and thrive;

Re - fresh-ing showers of grace di-vine, From Je-sus flow to eve - ry vine, And make the dead re - vive, And make the dead re - vive. vive.

O that this dry and barren ground
In springs of water may abound,
A fruitful soil become,
A fruitful soil become.
The desert blossoms as the rose,
While Jesus conquers all His foes,
And makes His people one,
And makes His people one.

Come, brethren, ye that love the Lord,
Who taste the sweetness of His word,
In Jesus' ways go on,
In Jesus' ways go on.
Our troubles and our trials here
Will only make us richer there,
When we arrive at home,
When we arrive at home.

A Sett of Jiggs

Key of G

Henry Purcell
Apollo's Banquet, H. Playford 1690
arr. © Hesperus

Recorder variation, last part of Jigg V

Last Time D.S.

m. 14   mm. 43-44

Scotch Cap

Key of D dorian
Original key of B dorian

The Dancing Master
arr. © Hesperus

Originally a lively country dance, "Scotch Cap" has been transformed by Scott into a slow dulcimer air.

The Merry Milkmaids

Key of C

The Dancing Master
arr. © Hesperus

Some Variations of B

Fiddle Harmonies

The President's March

Key of D

Philip Phile
arr. © Hesperus

We found the "President's March" (referring to George Washington) and "Ça Ira" (the French revolutionary call to arms) printed on the same sheet of paper from 18th-century Philadelphia; a further testimony to the political sympathy between the Americans and the French.

Ça Ira

French Traditional
arr. © Hesperus

Key of G

The Swallow

Key of G

First Book of Cotillions
arr. © Hesperus

This is the only time that Scott plays an accompaniment exactly as it appears in the printed version. The printed score was probably intended for the pianoforte which, when you think about it, is really just a mechanized hammered dulcimer anyway.

The Colly Flower

Key of G/G minor

First Book of Cotillions
arr. © Hesperus

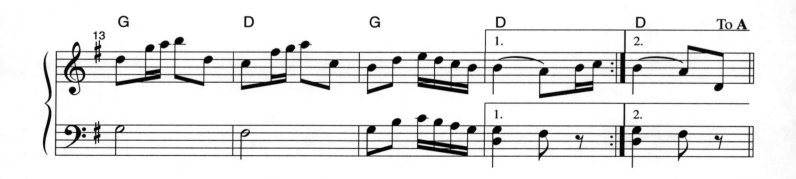

The "Colly Flower" is in rondo form: the first section is a refrain which comes back after each subsequent strain. In addition we made the "Swallow" and the "Colly Flower" into a mini-rondo by returning to the "Swallow" after the "Colly Flower" was finished. Tina enjoys varying the first section upon repetition.

Johnny Cock thy Beaver
a *Scotch* Tune to a Ground

Key of G

The Division Violin
arr. © Hesperus

Fiddle Countermelody

A beaver is a hat.

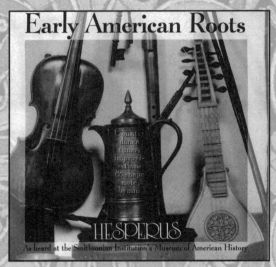